Get Well,
Pug

Read all the Diary of a Pug books!

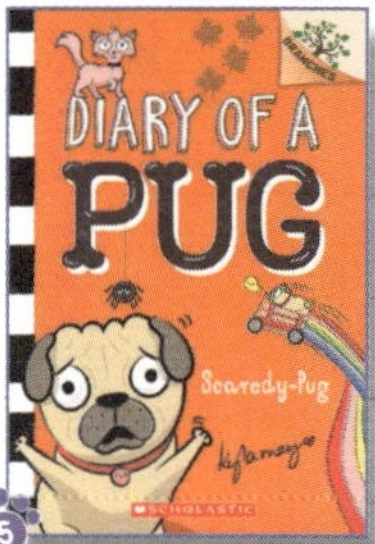

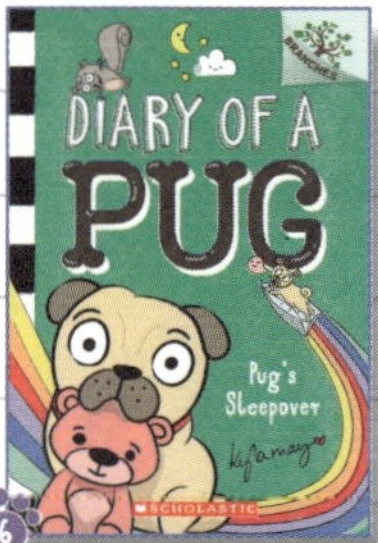

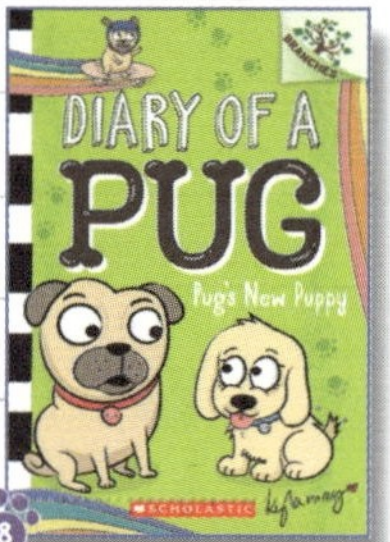

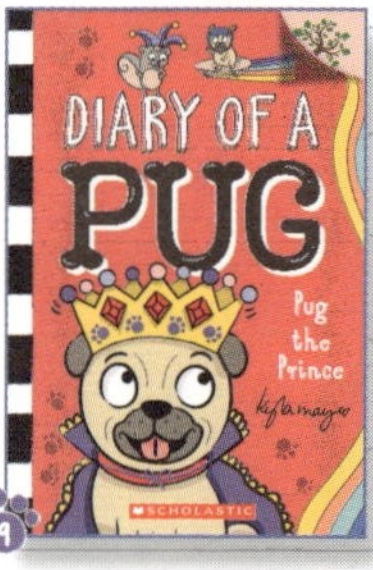

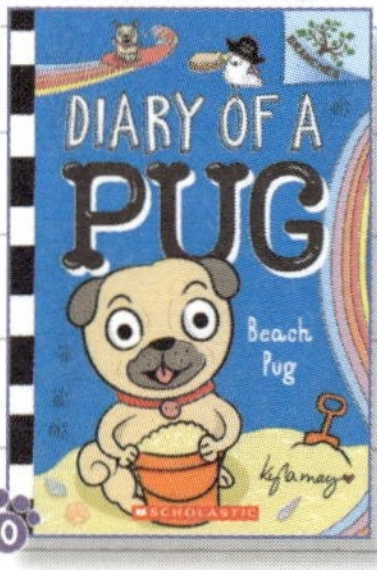

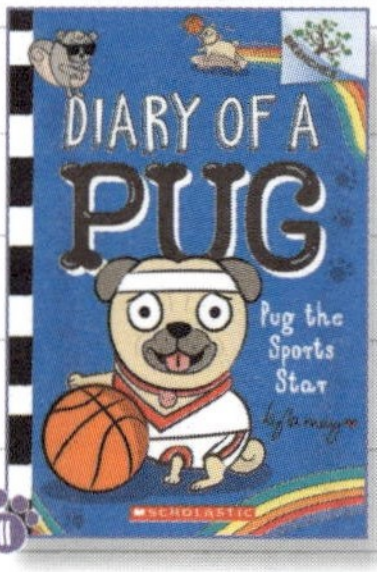

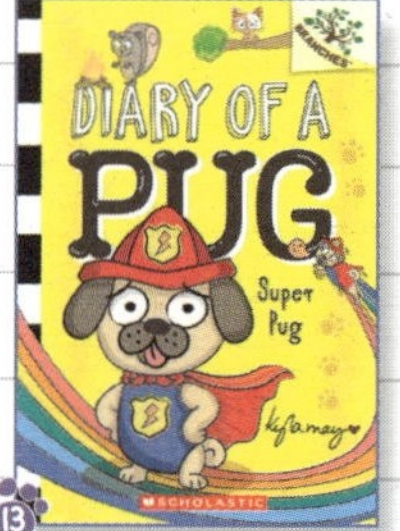

More books coming soon!

DIARY OF A PUG

Get Well, Pug

By Kyla May

SCHOLASTIC INC.

I dedicate this book to my talented creative daughter Mikka, who I love so much.

Special thanks to Meredith Rusu

Library of Congress Cataloging-in-Publication Data
Names: May, Kyla, author, illustrator.
Title: Get well, pug / by Kyla May.
Description: First edition. | New York : Branches/Scholastic Inc., 2025. |
Series: Diary of a pug ; 12 | Audience: Ages 5–7. | Audience: Grades
K–1. | Summary: When Bub's injury forces him to wear a cone, Duchess and
Luna must convince him to overcome his embarrassment so he can perform in Bella's pet choir.
Subjects: LCSH: Pug—Juvenile fiction. | Animals—Juvenile fiction. |
Embarrassment—Juvenile fiction. | Diaries—Juvenile fiction. | Humorous
stories. | CYAC: Pug—Fiction. | Dogs—Fiction. | Animals—Fiction. |
Embarrassment—Fiction. | Diaries—Fiction. | Humorous stories. | LCGFT:
Animal fiction. | Humorous fiction. | Diary fiction.

ISBN 978-93-5954-525-7

This reprint edition: July 2025
Edited by AnnMarie Anderson
Book design by Kyla May and Christian Zelaya

Printed in India MicroPrints India, New Delhi

Table of Contents

WELL REHEARSED

SATURDAY

Dear Diary,

Guess what? I'm going to have a solo in Bella's Pet Choir!

I'll fill you in on the details. But first, here are some things to know about me. I'm a dog of many talents.

I make many different faces:

Showtime Face

Starstruck Face

I Tooted Onstage Face

These are some of my favorite things:

BELLA SNUGGLES

PLAYTIME WITH LUNA

SURPRISE PEANUT BUTTER TREATS

Here are some things that get on my nerves:

DUCHESS

Warm milk is much better for your voice than toilet water.

I don't drink from the toilet!

NUTZ

Did I ever tell you about my days performing with the Treetop Trio?

And **WATER**. I hate getting wet!

It's funny because that's how I got my full name. Once, Bella was taking a bubble bath. I jumped in, too. But I didn't know there was water UNDER the bubbles! Bella named me **BARON VON BUBBLES** after that.

Now back to my story. Bella's scout troop is holding a music festival next weekend.

Some of the scouts are singing.

Some scouts are playing instruments.

A few are even making their own style of music.

But Bella taught me, Duchess, and Luna to bark and meow in time to a song she wrote. We're Bella's Pet Choir! And we've been preparing all month.

Bella even built a practice stage in her backyard. The best part is that at the end of our song, I have my own beatbarking solo! (That's a fancy way of saying I can bark in a cool rhythm.)

Everyone sounds great!
All we need now are stage outfits.

What are stage outfits?

They're the fancy clothes you wear onstage for the performance.

I didn't know we'd get to wear stage outfits, Diary. Since I have a solo, mine should be EXTRA special!

Bella showed Jack, Luna, Duchess, and me a few choices.

But I disagreed. My solo is a big deal. And I want to look perfect!

You look like the star of the show, Bubby!

I think so, too!

The music festival is one week away. I can't wait to shine!

Chapter 2

WELL . . . WELP!

SUNDAY

Dear Diary,

At today's rehearsal, Luna, Duchess, and I sounded better than ever.

I was feeling PUMPED! I jumped and wiggled around to show Bella how excited I was.

You're really feeling the star power, aren't you?

Bub, you're so silly!

The star power made me feel like I could fly! I leapt off the stage. And that's when the unthinkable happened . . .

Ouch!
Oh no! Bub, are you okay?
Ow, ow, ow, ow, ow!
This looks bad.
We need to get you to the vet.

Bella hurried to get her mom.
Meanwhile, Luna tried to cheer me up.

What's the Big, Bad Cone?
Oh, it's the big plastic cone dogs wear when they get hurt.
Like an ice-cream cone?
No. Not like an ice-cream cone. It warns other dogs not to be foolish and get hurt, too.
But it was an accident!

I had never heard of the Big, Bad Cone. It sounded terrible. What did it look like? Would it go on my leg? Or on my whole body?

What was going to happen, Diary? Would I really need the Big, Bad Cone?

GET WELL, PUG

MONDAY

Dear Diary,

I have good news and bad news. The good news is the vet said my leg will heal in a few weeks. And it doesn't hurt as much anymore. The bad news is . . .

I got the Big, Bad Cone just like Duchess said!

Let me tell you how it happened. We went to the vet. There were lots of other pets there, too. Some were hurt like me. Others were sick.

Squawk!
Broke my wing!
Broke my wing!

The people in the waiting room petted me. One lady even gave me a peanut butter snack. So far, being at the vet wasn't as scary as I thought it would be.

Then it was my turn to see the vet. He didn't have any peanut butter treats. But he was nice.

When the vet showed us the X-ray, it wasn't good news.

The cone wasn't what I had imagined. It was just a plastic collar. But I still didn't like it!

Now here I am, with the Big, Bad Cone just like Duchess said. It's so annoying!

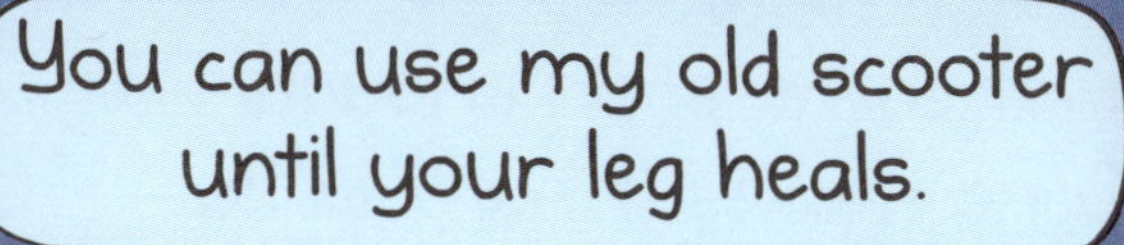
You can use my old scooter until your leg heals.
I know it's frustrating. But you'll get well in no time!

"No time" can't come soon enough, Diary. The Big, Bad Cone makes it hard to do anything well.

So, you got the
Big, Bad Cone after all, huh?
It's to protect my cast.
Not to warn other dogs.
But it's still the worst.

I can't go onstage with the Big, Bad Cone, Diary! I'll look ridiculous! What am I going to do?

WELL, I'M OUT!

TUESDAY

Dear Diary,

Bella said that at today's rehearsal I can practice beatbarking in my cone.

But I still wasn't sure doing the show with the Big, Bad Cone was a good idea.

For the love of tuna,
it's not an ice-cream cone.
It's just the Big, Bad Cone.

To make matters worse, Nutz overheard us. He started asking questions.

I AM NOT AN ICE-CREAM CONE!
Big. Bad. Cone.

Oh, yeah. I've heard about these cones.
They're to warn other dogs not to get hurt, too, right?
Told you.
I guess your solo will be entertaining and educational then, Bubster.

THAT'S IT! I'm leaving!
Relax, Bubbykins. We're just kidding.
BELLA'S PET CHOIR
Your solo will still sound fine. No one cares about the cone.
I CARE! I'm supposed to look perfect onstage!

Bub, what's wrong?
Aren't you going to be in my pet choir?

No, no, no, no, NO!

Diary, there was no way I was performing with the silly Big, Bad Cone. I wanted to stand out—but not like this!

Chapter 5

HOWL-WELL-ING

WEDNESDAY

Dear Diary,

Today, Bella tried to convince me to perform. But my answer was still "No!"

Without Bub's beatbarking solo, my pet choir doesn't have a finale.

Is his leg still hurting him?

I don't know. Maybe? He doesn't want to get onstage.

BELLA'S PET CHOIR

Why don't you want to perform, Bub?
Isn't it obvious?
I don't look like a star
when I'm wearing this cone.
It's not that bad.
Yes, it is! This thing is actually
called the Big, BAD Cone!

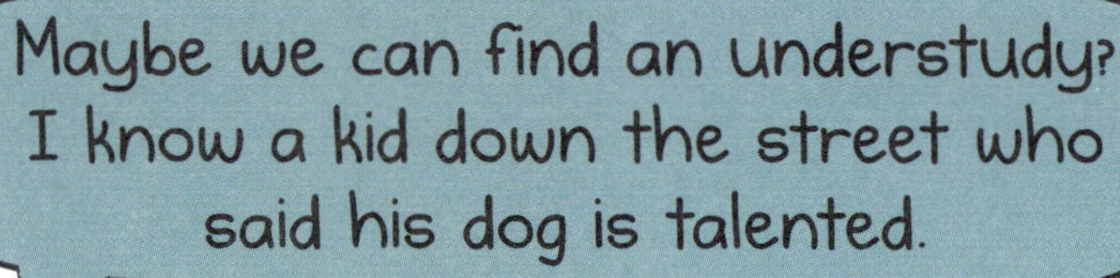
Maybe we can find an understudy? I know a kid down the street who said his dog is talented.
Really? Okay—let's give it a try.
What's an understudy, Luna?
It's a showbiz word. It means another dog will take your place because you can't perform.

Could Bella find another dog to replace me, Diary? Just like that?

Jack returned a few minutes later.

Just follow along for now, Von Trapp.
And a one, and a two . . .
Woof, woof, woof.
Meow, meow, meow.
BELLA'S PET CHOIR
Your turn, Von Trapp. Let's hear it!

HOOOOW—WOOOODLE—WAAAAY WEEEEE—WOOOOOO!
That's not beatbarking! That's yodel-howling!

I probably should have mentioned that. Von Trapp is more of a yodel-howler than a beatbarker.
It's okay. He did great!
We'll figure out a way to make this song work . . . somehow.
BELLA'S PET CHOIR

I can't perform under these conditions! Bub, remind me WHY you aren't performing again?

Hello! Big, Bad Cone, remember?

I felt bad about messing up the whole show, Diary. But I couldn't go onstage looking so un-star like.

Do you think Bella can make the song work with Von Trapp instead?

Chapter 6

WILL IT GO WELL?

THURSDAY

Dear Diary,

Von Trapp tried his best during today's rehearsal, but he had trouble staying on the beat.

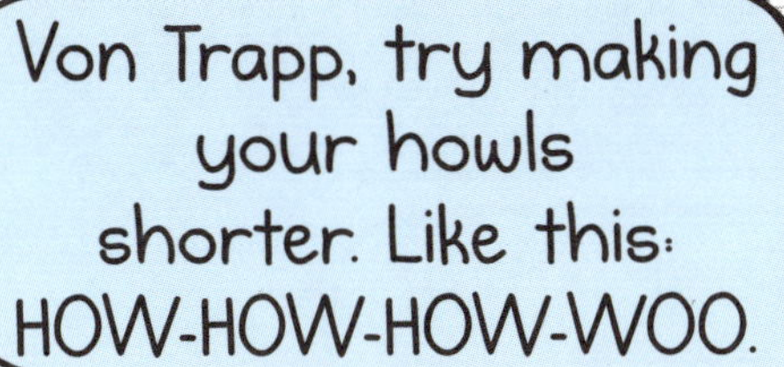

Diary, rehearsal was not going well.

Your yodel-howl sounds great. It's my song that's the problem.
I wrote it to end with a beatbark solo, not a yodel.
Maybe you could rewrite it?
There's not enough time. We'll practice it again.

While Bella, Jack, and Tommy went inside to get us some snacks, I gave Von Trapp some pointers to help him sound more beatbark-y.

Yeah, Bub. Why AREN'T you in the show again?
Because I look like an ice-cream cone, not a star.
And I told YOU, no one cares what you look like. They want to hear you bark, not see your outfit sparkle.

But what if people say I look silly?
Just ignore them.
Cats ignore people all the time.
Only YOU can do your solo.
Just do you. Everyone will love it.

Why are you being nice to me?

Honestly? The song doesn't sound the same without you.

I mean, it sounds OKAY without you. But it sounds GREAT with you. I need YOU to make ME look good!

Maybe Duchess is right. Diary, should I perform in Bella's Pet Choir after all?

SOUNDING SWELL

FRIDAY

Dear Diary,

It's a brand-new day and I've made my decision: I'm going to bark in the show tomorrow, cone and all!

Bella was so happy when she saw me onstage again.

Don't worry, Von Trapp. You're still in my choir, too! I have a new idea that's going to be great.

We got ready to rehearse one last time. But after everything that had happened, would we sound okay?

And Bub, take it away!

I had done it, Diary! I sang my solo with the cone and everything. It didn't matter what I looked like. I still sounded like a real singing star! In fact . . .

Bub! Your cone is like a beatbarking megaphone. It makes your solo sound better than ever!

Hmmm . . . what if we made your cone part of the show?

But how?

Just because your sparkly outfit won't fit over your cast doesn't mean you can't shine!
We can decorate your cone so it's one-of-a-kind!
I LOVE that idea!

We spent the rest of the afternoon making new snazzy stage outfits for all of us — with my cone for inspiration.

Who would have thought, Diary? The show will go on after all!

Chapter 8

ALL'S WELL THAT ENDS WELL

SATURDAY

Dear Diary,

The big day was finally here. It was showtime!

The minute the spotlight came on, I felt so nervous I could toot. Everyone was looking at me.

Duchess was right. I took a deep breath . . .

And we rocked our performance!

WOOF, WOOF, WOOFA-WOOF WOOF. WOOFA-WOOFA WOOF, WOOF, WOOF!
Wooooooo . . .

The crowd loved us! Everyone cheered and hollered. I felt so happy.

You were right, Duchess.
No one cared about my cone!
I know. I'm always right.
Thanks for convincing
me to sing after all.
After all that hard work,
we deserved to sound great.

I was so proud, Diary. Being in Bella's Pet Choir wasn't about how I looked. It was about barking my heart out and being myself. Because no matter what—the show must go on! And it was even better with my friends by my side!

About the Creator

Kyla May is an Australian illustrator, writer, and designer. In addition to books, Kyla creates animation. She lives by the beach in Victoria, Australia, with her three daughters, two cats, and two dogs. Bub the Pug was inspired by her daughter's pug.

HOW MUCH DO YOU KNOW ABOUT

DIARY OF A PUG

Get Well, Pug

What is an x-ray?
Reread page 25.

Bella makes me peanut butter doggie pancakes after my vet visit. How would you cheer up a sick or injured friend?

I tell Bub the Big, Bad Cone is a warning to other dogs. What is it really for? Reread page 26.

I join Bella's Pet Choir as Bub's understudy. What is an understud
Reread page 44.

Get creative! Draw a new stage outfit for Bub. Include his cone ir your design.

scholastic.com/branches